MY EVERYDAY TAGALOG WORDS
WITH NATHAN & JOHN

WRITTEN BY CARLOS CABANEROS
ILLUSTRATED BY REZA RAY

Kids of Today Inc.

New York – Manila – Toronto – Dubai – Tokyo – Riyadh – London – Paris – Beijing – Seoul – Moscow – Berlin – Rome – Singapore

Copyright © 2021 by Kids of Today Inc.

John is Filipino, he is from the Philippines. He immigrated to Canada at a young age. Nathan is his best friend who was born and raised in Canada. Nathan asked John if he can teach him some Tagalog words.

"Can you teach me Tagalog, John?"

"Of course! Are you ready to learn Nathan?"

"Yes, I am!"

"Let's go!"

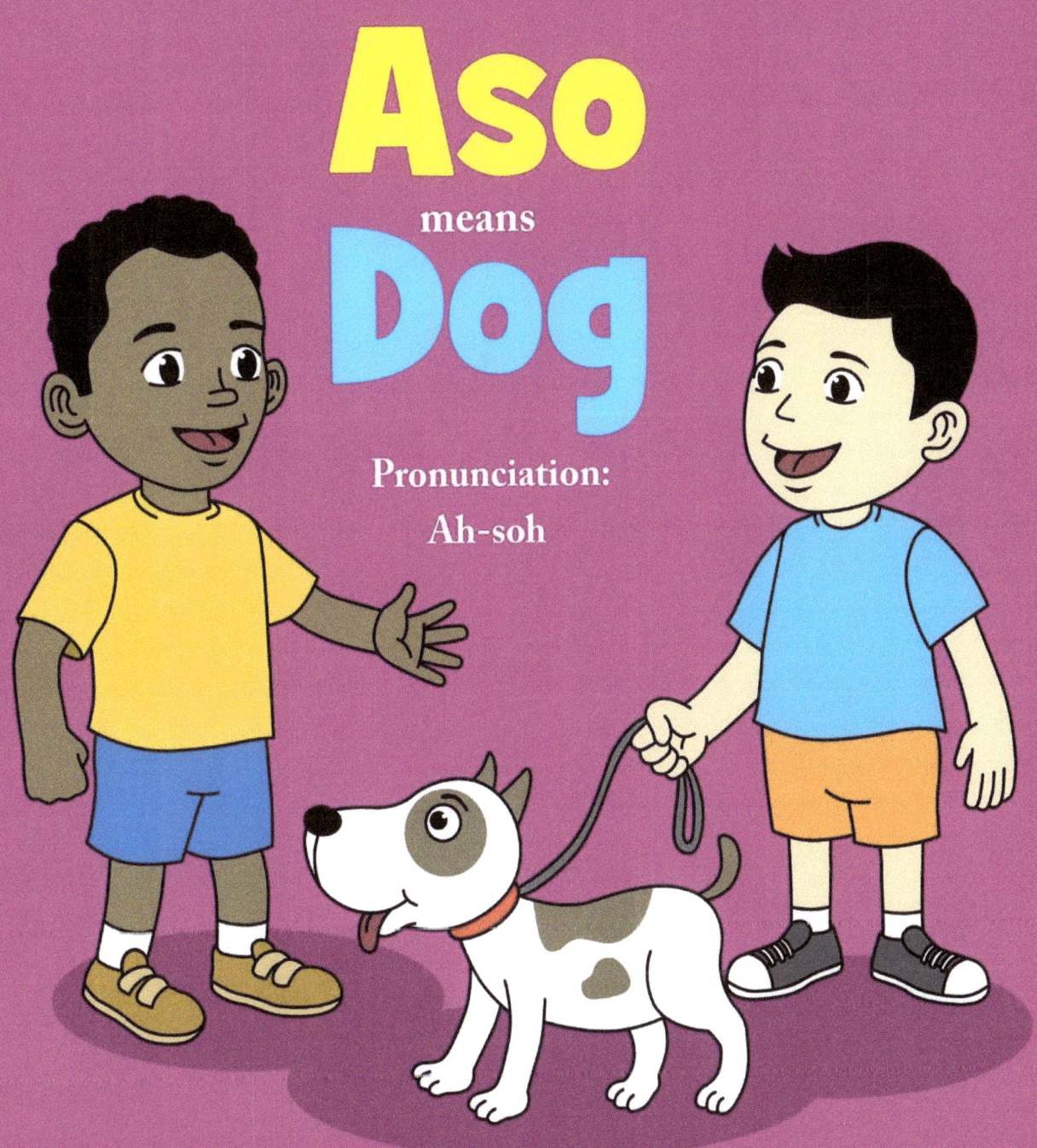

Aso means Dog

Pronunciation: Ah-soh

Eg. Sentence:
We love our aso, he is playful and lovable towards my family and I.

Apoy
means
Fire

Pronunciation:
Ah-poy

Eg. Sentence:
Burning wood to make us apoy to warm us in the winter cold.

Bahay means House

Pronunciation: Bah-hai

Eg. Sentence:

My bahay has different rooms, and a special room for me to play with my toys.

Baso
means
Cup

Pronunciation: Bah-soh

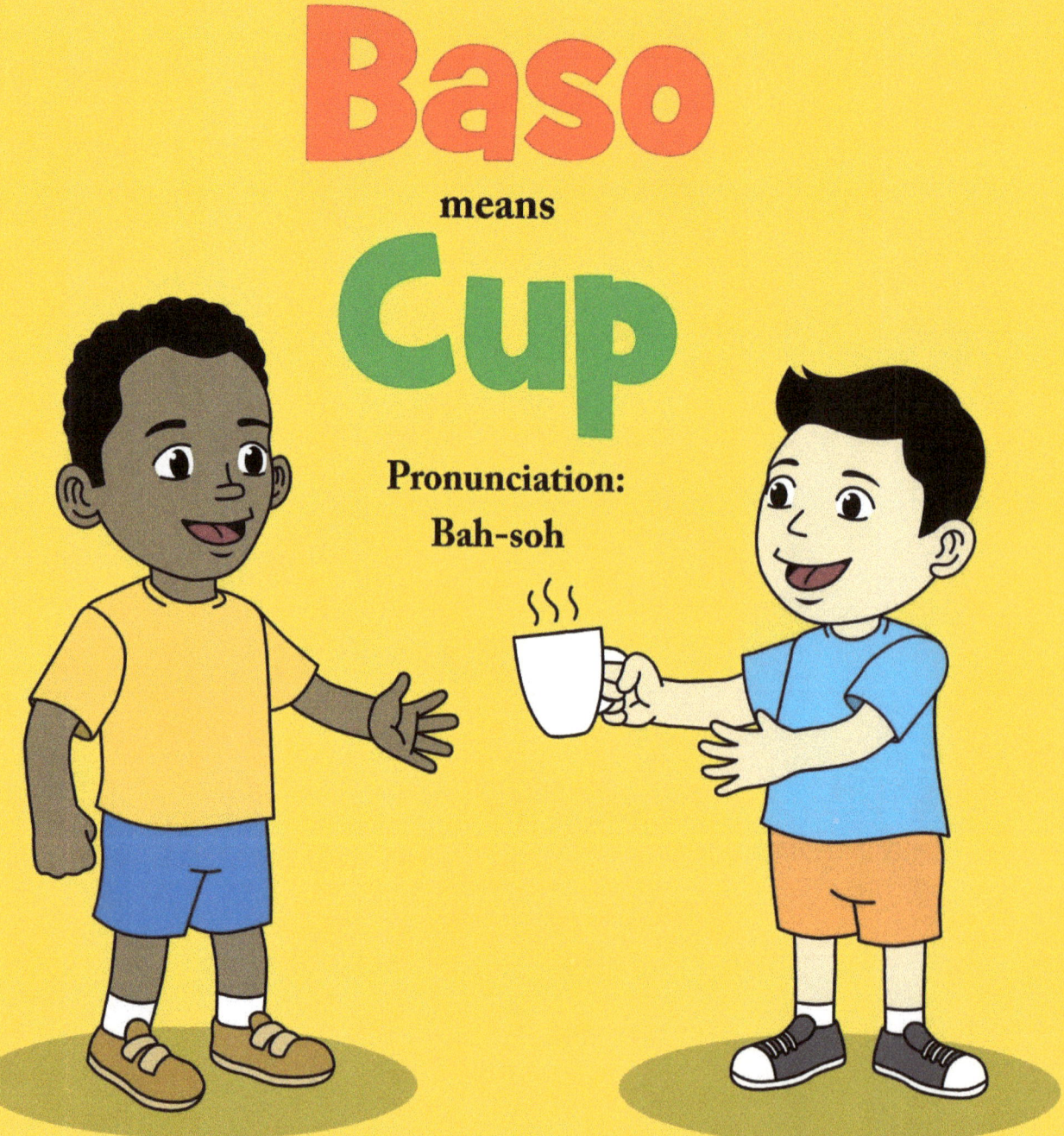

Eg. Sentence:
I love to drink hot chocolate in my favourite Christmas baso.

Damit
means
Clothes

Pronunciation:
Duh-met

Eg. Sentence:
Today I am wearing my favourite damit.

Eroplano
means
Airplane

Pronunciation:
Eh-roh-plano

Eg. Sentence:
I like riding on an eroplano to travel to different countries.

Elepante means Elephant

Pronunciation:
Eh-leh-pan-teh

Eg. Sentence:
An elepante is so big, I would love to see one in real life.

Gunting
means
Scissors

Pronunciation:
Goon-ting

Eg. Sentence:
I use my gunting for my arts and crafts.

Halaman
means
Plants

Pronunciation:
Hah-lah-mah-n

Eg. Sentence:
Watering my pot of halaman every morning keeps it green and healthy.

Hagdan

means

Ladder/stairs

Pronunciation:
Hug-dan

Eg. Sentence:
I climb the hagdan with my mom to go to my room.

Ibon means Birds

Pronunciation:
Ee-Bon

Eg. Sentence:
Blue ibon, like the blue jays, fly high in the sky.

Ilong
means
Nose

Pronunciation:
ee-long

Eg. Sentence:
I use my ilong to smell all my favourite foods.

Kama
means
Bed

Pronunciation:
Kah-mah

Eg. Sentence:
My Kama is soft and comfortable.

Kamiseta
means
Shirt

Pronunciation:
Kah-mih-syetah

Eg. Sentence:
I have my favourite kamiseta for going outside to play.

Lapis
means
Pencil

Pronunciation:
Lah-pis

Eg. Sentence:
I use my lapis to draw.

Lola
means
Grandmother

Pronunciation:
Loh-la

Eg. Sentence:
My lola makes the best food.

Mata
means
Eyes

Pronunciation: Mah-tah

Eg. Sentence:
We use our mata to see the beautiful world we live in.

Medyas
means
Socks

Pronunciation:
Med-yas

Eg. Sentence:
Wearing medyas keep your feet warm and comfy.

Nanay means Mother

Pronunciation:
Na-nay

Eg. Sentence:
I have the best nanay in the world.

Niyog
means
Coconut

Pronunciation:
Nee-Yog

Eg. Sentence:
Niyog only grows in tropical countries. They are very delicious.

Oras
means
Time

16.05

Pronunciation:
Oh-rahs

Eg. Sentence:
I have to remember the oras to get to school on time.

Puno
means
Tree

Pronunciation:
Poo-noh

Eg. Sentence:
There is a big green puno at the park.

Pusa
means
Cat

Pronunciation:
Poo-sah

Eg. Sentence:
My pet pusa loves to sleep.

Relo
means
Watch

Pronunciation:
Reh-loh

Eg. Sentence:
I look at my relo to see the time.

Salamin
means
Glass

Pronunciation:
Sah-lah-mean

Eg. Sentence:
While I brush my teeth, I look at myself in the salamin.

Suklay
means
Comb/hair brush

Pronunciation:
Sook-lai

Eg. Sentence:
Using my blue suklay when my hair is messy.

Tatay means Father

Pronunciation:
Tah-tahy

Eg. Sentence:
My tatay always plays fun games with me.

Telepono
means
Telephone

Pronunciation:
Te-le-poh-noh

Eg. Sentence:
I use the telepono to call my friends.

Ulap means Clouds

Pronunciation: Ooo-lap

Eg. Sentence:
There are so many ulap in the sky today.

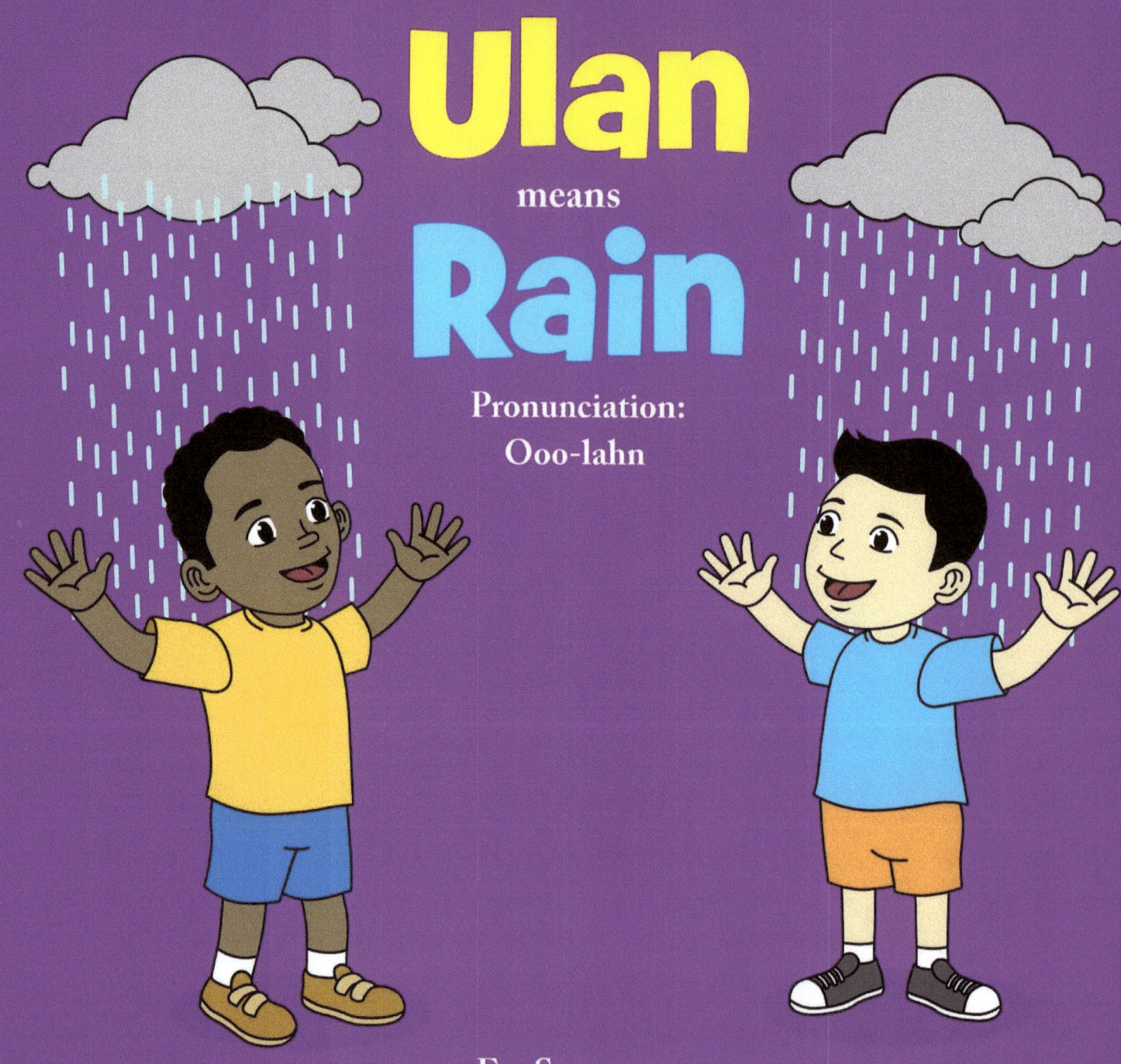

Walis
means
Broom

Pronunciation:
Wa-lis

Eg. Sentence:
I use a walis to sweep the floor.

Yeso
means
Chalk

Pronunciation:
Yeh-soh

Eg. Sentence:
Sometimes during recess my friends and I play with yeso.

Copyright © 2021 by Kids of Today Inc.

All rights reserved. No part of this publication may be reproduced, distributed, or transmitted in any form or by any means, including photocopying, recording, or other electronic or mechanical methods, without the prior written permission of the publisher, except in the case of brief quotations embodied in critical reviews and certain other noncommercial uses permitted by copyright law. For permission requests, write to the publisher, addressed "Attention: Permissions Coordinator," at the address below.

kidsoftodayinc@gmail.com

www.ingramcontent.com/pod-product-compliance
Lightning Source LLC
Chambersburg PA
CBHW061127170426
43209CB00014B/1685